A Parable of Women:

Poems

Philip C. Kolin

Yazoo River Press
2009

Acknowledgments

I gratefully acknowledge the following publications in which some of the poems in this collection originally appeared:

"Hagar's Lament." *The Penwood Review* 7.1 (2003): 12.

"Her Last Photo." *Theology Today* [Princeton Univ.] 61 (2004): 362.

"Midlife." *Louisiana Literature* 24 (2007): 79.

"The Singles Again Party." *Valley Voices* 7.2 (2007): 37.

"The Nun in the Prayer Room." *Motel 58* [Virginia] (2009).

"Mary's Aria." *The Penwood Review* 11.1 (2007): 39.

Yazoo River Press
14000 Hwy 82 West, #5032
Itta Bena, MS 38941-1400

Cover art: *The Holy Women at the Sepulchre* (1614). Oil on Panel. Peter Paul Rubens.

Table of Contents

A House Without Doors

She told me to look for
A house without doors

Always open or
Always closed?

The answer was
In exits and entrances

They always share
The same room—

One half life
One half eternity.

Hagar's Lament

My son was
More destined than
Any of the caravan children
Suckled on the thistle
Milk of coarse-browed maids
Who found his favor
Only once
And then left
To journey through
His adopted land,
Orphaned.

My son was cool sunlight
In his father's eye
Laughter gamboled with
Time's potency to voice
The capture of age
By my womb's desire.

My bonds were
Love's trinkets
Shackles to hold his eye
The time was free for us
We coupled with the law.
My son under Sinai
Played a tabor while
His father slept

But not restfully.
Nightly his calls to me
Fretted with the aches
Of a man uncomfortable
With his flesh
His kindness wandered

He heard Sarah
As if God spoke

Violets and jasmine on her lips—
An old garden for his treasure.

The other one looked to me
Pale as bread
And I in my prime
Took the salty wilderness
As my consort—a covenant of arrows
Flailed my heart
I hid my pride.

But God opened
My eyes to wells
Deeper than the Red Sea:
My son's sons all darkened
In the promise that baptized
The offspring she weaned
In the shadows of my tent.

The Wicker Basket

The wicker basket
Wedged on the bottom shelf
Of the guest bedroom
Marks my life passage.

It is a funeral home of photos
Of ancestors whose names
And faces I cannot connect
To who I am or was.

As I dig in the basket
I am in a bottomless coffin
Of uncles of uncles
A row of pomaded nephews
Whose heirs may or may not be gone.

A veil of silver nitrate coats
The faces of my ghostly relatives
Men's faces buried
Beneath thick, burly beards
Women sewn into the frocks
Of childbirth. But whose?

These curled photos don't
Unravel names. Not me or
My mother but maybe
Hers or hers or hers
This genealogy of my lost

Family caught in the outdoors
On picnics with
Nickel pails of beer
In Chicago forest preserves
Or on the steps of streaked churches
Forefathers whose high stiff collars
Stop them from calling out
Who they are.

These mute dead are imprisoned
Between the wooden slats
On a voyage I will have to take
Someday.

Her Last Photo

The day she entered the convent
Her father clicked her
Picture: head titled up
Just to the right,
A pose welcoming the flash
Of light courting her—this new
Woman—through the lens.

On her lips
An infinity of smiles
As if she were told
A secret that left
Others perplexed.

Her eyes wrote sweet notes
To those who read only sad
Stories all around them.

Her hands were
Porcelain prayers
White and spotless
Ready for grace
To be emptied into them.

She would leave
The busy garden background—
This world of noisy seasons

For choired silence and
Cloistered flowers.

My Cousin

A soft shadow across the park pool
My cousin dove into water that never parted
She slid smoothly in.

But her friends taunted her
To jump from the pool house—
Over nine feet high, and ten far feet away
Into the pool, after
Hours.

For these Olympics, her sister awarded
Her silence, and echoed it back to
My uncle and aunt, satisfied
That their younger daughter listened.

But she kept diving into smaller
And smaller pools
Less and less
Unguarded by the light
Until she drowned inside
A teardrop.

Edith

I was the youngest
Of three sisters
Slight, shadowy, thinking
Always alone
I wore a thin floral dress
And a shallow smile
My shoulders frowned.

Had I not died
You would have never
Known that I was
More quotidian than
Doing supper dishes.

I saw ghosts ahead of time
In our family album
My sisters wore wings
Our mother's hands cupped
Blue, billowy pillows.

I wanted a lover
And imitated every sigh
I heard in the cinema until
He came one night and took
The *nom de plume* of Pneumonia
Embracing me in a slow trance...

The wheezing was
Suicide's language of swooning.

My contribution to life
Was my obituary
Finally a notice
Of who I was close-up yet
A dowager's three flower car procession
Overshadowed me.

I play solitaire in purgatory.

Magdalen

Again tears reigned
In her eyes running
Ahead of the horizon

She expected death—
Pressed linen
In a sealed
Alabastered tomb,
The sad security of stone.

There before her
The laughter of angels
Sprung the snares of time.

Her life sighed
A history of touch
Her hair, his feet

Who keeps a garden
In a grave
Robbers, she thought,
As she turned

She saw the one
Whose caress
She would never feel
The same again.

Midlife

It's high summer
July, a moon almost ripe
The beach is tender tonight
Winds like sweet basil rouge
Give our faces
A glow, erasing years of wear.

Time is a companionable griot
Recounting stories of loves possible.

The sand along the shoreline
Runs a pleasant course
The surf is a sieve—
Wanting and wasting
Cancel each other out:
The perfect equipoise
Of an hourglass always turned.

Orange and yellow lights
On every porch or above
The condo balconies
Flicker like votive candles

To a kind desire
Mellow, at midlife, now
Comfortable, predictable, assured.

Your hand reaches for mine.
A smile for our walk—
A steady surprise.

Over Coffee

She wanted to see him
Over coffee they could
Work things out
All the problems
That stirred their marriage.

Just a few minutes
From his busy day

Part of his lunch
Time to meet
Her expectations

Too high he thought
As she started filling in
What went right
What went wrong—
A crossworded puzzle.

He touched his watch
A parole to free him
For the rest of the day

From her that night
He flirts with
Four or five St. Pauli Girls
At Headlines, a sports bar

Across town
She wraps up
The coffee grinds
In yesterday's want ads

And throws them
Out.

Cha Cha Blues

She was in a decade long marriage
Do a full basic

But never had the children she longed for
Do a half basic

Then she met a suave, dark dancer
Now do a crossover

She fell for his wooing and fell to cheating
Here comes the chase

This new man promised her a fruitful womb
Rock on the inside foot for a sweetheart step

She thought they discovered love
Glide into the swivel

She told the ten-year husband goodbye
Keep right foot pointed for backflick

The dancing lover came right in
Keep your arc for half moon

Just a few months later this new dancer left her
Now do a crossover

Pregnant and without a lover or a husband
End with flirtation.

The Singles Again Party

She arrives at the party
And again
She puts her youth on

Just right,
Her cheeks are glazed
Like late fall snow.

She hopes her lip gloss will seal off
Any more Judas kisses
From men whose promises glitter
Like 30 cubic zirconium.

She is ready for the rules of engagement
Armed with a trinity of comforts—
Xanax, mints, and Zoloft.

As she steps into the mirror
She won't allow memory
To be hostage to fear
She's a real bella donna now.

The room is skewed
Toward the door and windows,
Escapes for all eyes
That have not discovered
Someone worth a second glance.

Her looks sweep across
The floor like a vacuum cleaner
Picking up only
The most magnetic faces.

All but one are
Already coupled
Too late

He is gone—
The other smiles are occupied
No refuge for her words.

On her way out
She picks up a bloated carrot
And dips it in the ghostly
Ranch dressing.

Herodias Throws A Party

I like swank, chic, class
Always go Bobbie Brooks, Jack LaLanne, Coach
I revel in making sure people understand
My connections—brother, brother-in-law, father are
All the same—powerful men with ravenous selves.

Just the other day, you might like to know,
I introduced a fashionable local abortionist
To several of my Botoxed friends.
He gave them his business card—New Beginnings, LP.
An unwanted pregnancy—ugh; all those extra pounds
Just unthinkable. Children
Are fine but not at the wrong time,
Especially Christmas. Who needs it?

Don't you love these mirrored walls
We get a chance to reinvent ourselves.

I've spent a tetrarch's ransom on Salome
So she can unveil the latest gowns.
Have you seen her this season?
She stays so busy; she always turns heads.
My therapy, I suspect, is her sin!

One bolero with her
And a man catches on fire
Like an Art Deco bungalow
In a Santa Ana wind.

Pardon me. Good news at last.
The first platter is coming in.
It's a delicacy to kill for.

I am so discomforted by waiting.

Latitudes

She travels to Rio, Recife,
And Santiago de Cuba
Three nights a week

On the breathless floor boards
Of the Methodist church cafeteria
Her crow's-feet do Ponce de Leon steps.

She sways away
Wrinkles, Bengay aches,
Two bulging divorces
And her Atkins held over
Pounds.

For ten dollars per Latin cruise
She flirts with her fantasies—
She is South America
On the map of desire

She caresses the dark palms
Of Africa who kisses her from the east
She inhales the deep percussion of
Perez Prado's Caballa Negro.

And from the south
She woos with fire
Her glacial partner
North America, melting
Down in latitudes to her.

She seasons the air
With salsa and merengue
Trapped on Anglo nights
In covered dish socials.

She spins so passionately
The moon runs out of breath.

Moths

In the summer she leaves
The little yellow light on all night
On her back porch

A palette of moths
Paints the glass
On the door

Embroidering a history of tongues,
Wings, assignations.

When opened—if only
Briefly—a few fly
Inside the canvas

Like the strokes
Of a fresco master
Before he makes them public

The fluorescent light
Above her stove
Scorches his creation.

Wondra's Dolor Bills

Wondra is as thin
As a stringy, worn shoelace
She's a waitress by day
By night a waitress
Who's got time for time
Off in the ghetto where everyone is
Bi-lingual—misery and worry
Are the vocabulary de jour.

Her boss pays her in spite
Of the past due notices
That starve her purse.

Her body's Biblical
Sort of Noah inside out
Fish living in her belly,
Feeding off the nutrients
Of hope and sight.

History's got her wrong.
Who says she's free and clear?
The 13th Amendment means
No more to her than
A wink to a hearse rider.

Maybe next year
She will get on
At Wal-Mart Plantation.

Odeila's House

Do not demolish me
Cries the house from
Behind shorn shutters
On Last Esperanza St.

In the Lower Ninth. It was
On the city's tombstone list
Before she knew
Her dreams had died.

Her family was legacied
On a foundation of photos
Without any walls now
To hold them

She has been sent away
To an orphanage of air.

Her house was a husband who stood up
For her on dark nights.
The rafters on the street
Are his remains

Waiting
To be picked up.

The Lady of the Viaduct

She lives in
The underhistory of the city

Under its bridges
Under its impasses
Under its rushing, crushing
18 bully wheelers
Under its standing
Under its indifference
That she still lives at all.

She carries the voices of her life
In Sam Walton valises.

There was no place for her
In the shelters full of others
Whose timing was
Better than hers.

She sleeps tonight
On a concrete couch
In her cardboard boudoir.

Her lullaby will be
The sound of asphalt
Peeling away
Her dreams.

The Nun in the Prayer Room

She sits on the floor
In the corner,
Bundled like a fetus
Even in this out of the way place
He sees her great soul soaring.

I fidget with my mumbling
Spirit all caught up
In wayward words—
What if, how can
It be, why, if only. . .

Quietly she passes
Me a note here
In God's classroom.

"Stop putting starch
In every petition.
Relax your mea culpas
They are too stiff.
Bend your prayers
A little while.

He does not visit
This room to extract
Wails tonight."

His heralding might
Crouches in an old woman's smile.

The Widow's Waltz

On her mask of white bone
She lipsticked a smile but
No one had noticed her
All dance-evening long

Until gliding along came
A daffodildoed dandy
Three times younger
Than she was older
For a waltz or fox-trot.

She had practiced to the tune
Of Jesus loves me
This she knew
But now she had to

Join the long line of
The foot charade in their
Promenades and pirouettes
Across a gallery of fears

With artery-red streamers suspended
From the ballroom ceiling
Like the Paraclete's tongues
Calling her to high passion.

As he moved her
Against the grain
Of her halting rhythms
The faces on her watch ran
Backwards

From morphine nights, dripping
With the foggy breath of streetlamps
To the pale-sun morning
When her diagnosis dawned:

Lingering death or
Quick-stepped dreams
The dandy's yellow hand
Promised her both.

Running Out of Memory

She does not have enough memory
For retirement. Blank spaces
Fill her menu for life.

No one can fault her
She raised a three-child family
Her husband defaulted

On every promise.
She cannot recall
Even the outlines of his

Smiles and frowns
Are now synonymous
In her alphabet.

They keep track
Of her upstairs
In the records dept.

But she is running out
Of things to really live
Or die for.

Her insurance is limited
To the white sheet
That covers her.

Diane's Piano Studio

Choir boys skate across
The smooth white fields
She invites them to play on.
Between the rows of black
Fence poles they leave
Scores of laughing tracks—
Schumann smiles; Grieg giggles.

She conducts a symphony
Of butterflies, scattered
Like pieces of a rainbow,
In her sanctuary of ivory
And desire, coloring the air
With notes from Tchaikovsky.

At prayers she removes
The chromatic scales from her eyes
And opens the acacia ark
In her living room
To the proclamations of angels.

Winter's Piscary

The scratchy fingers of winter
Will not catch
These Ophelia spots of light
However much the half-moon
Maneuvers them into shadows.

The darkness resides
In the net,
Not the nymph.

Let our orisons not be
Circumferenced the same.
Mysteries too easily explained
Are kites escaping
While we hold onto
The tale.

Mary's Aria

I lay down with an angel's proposal
And awoke the spouse of a dove white whisper
That called to me in the starlight
To widen the way of wisdom.

I knew the names of the planets
The moment he was born
They sang their geometry to me
In canticles and comets.

My eyes pierced mysteries
That the patriarchs could not.

I learned that time was a thread in eternity
The earth just patched
The empty spaces.

At his first words
I saw the sun
Unfurl rainbow streamers
Full of pericopes
From Genesis and the Talmud.

The winds always cried
When we prayed at night
Every unborn holocausted soul
Petitioned us for
The kindness of rain,
Our tears.

My arms were the gates
For a sheepfold of pardons.

Now in my small stone house
In Ephesus a pale young man
Keeps a diary of my dreams
Revelations you will see some day.